Exploring Uncharted Vietnam

An 8-Day Expedition

Spondon Ganguli

Ukiyoto Publishing

All global publishing rights are held by

Ukiyoto Publishing

Published in 2024

Content Copyright © Spondon Ganguli

ISBN 9789362697929

All rights reserved.
No part of this publication may be reproduced,
transmitted, or stored in a retrieval system, in any
form by any means, electronic, mechanical,
photocopying, recording or otherwise, without the
prior permission of the publisher.

The moral rights of the author have been asserted.

This book is sold subject to the condition that it shall
not by way of trade or otherwise, be lent, resold, hired
out or otherwise circulated, without the publisher's
prior consent, in any form of binding or cover other
than that in which it is published.

www.ukiyoto.com

*I dedicate this book to my beloved daughter,
Aaditri Ganguli.*

Acknowledgement

With thanks I want to express my gratitude, for the blessings of a power that has given me the strength, knowledge, skills and chances to document my trip through Vietnam. This remarkable country has a history spanning a millennium, marked by periods of occupation and political turmoil. It emerges resilient from the shadows of the Vietnam War.

I want to thank all the people we met during our 8-day adventure in Vietnam. From the kind hotel managers to the restaurant owners, insightful tour guides and operators, cheerful cab drivers and lively street vendors—each individual added their touch to enrich this travel story. A special appreciation goes to Ms. Phi and her family as my Vietnamese friends on social media whose invitation allowed us to explore the beauty of their homeland—a journey I never imagined starting from Kolkata.

The crucial role played by Ukiyoto Publications in bringing this book to fruition cannot be emphasized enough. Their unwavering commitment and hard work have turned my dreams into a reality something, for which I'm deeply appreciative and thankful.

Spondon Ganguli

Prologue

What is a travelogue?

A travelogue is a piece of travel writing that is essentially about giving readers a sense of place in a way that is engaging, unique and inspiring in a way of capturing details and observations of own's travel including memories and other information to be shared with others.

Embarking on my first foreign journey outside the vibrant collage of India was a thrilling prospect, filled with a blend of excitement and anticipation. As an educator dedicated to unravelling the mysteries of knowledge and a passionate author weaving tales of inspiration, the prospect of delving into the enchanting landscapes and rich cultural heritage of Vietnam beckoned like a siren's call.

In the crisp autumn air of October 2018, my wife and I set foot on Vietnamese soil, ready to explore a land steeped in history, tradition, and natural splendour. Our itinerary promised a whirlwind adventure, spanning eight exhilarating days and encompassing four pivotal tourist hubs that encapsulated Vietnam's essence: Ho Chi Minh City, Hoi An, Ha Long Bay, and Hanoi.

The journey ahead held the promise of uncovering hidden gems, immersing ourselves in diverse cultural experiences, and forging unforgettable memories against the backdrop of Vietnam's picturesque landscapes. Each destination was a chapter waiting to be written, a canvas waiting to be painted with the vivid hues of discovery and exploration.

As we ventured forth, navigating bustling cityscapes, ancient towns steeped in heritage, and serene natural wonders, every step brought us closer to unravelling the intricacies of Vietnam's soul. From the pulsating energy of Ho Chi Minh City's bustling streets to the timeless allure of Hoi An's lantern-lit alleys, from the ethereal beauty of Ha Long Bay's emerald waters to the historical tapestry of Hanoi's ancient temples and bustling markets, our journey promised to be a tapestry of experiences woven with threads of wonder and awe.

Join me as we traverse the vibrant mosaic of Vietnam's landscapes, cultures, and traditions, delving deep into the heart of this captivating country and unravelling the secrets that lie within its storied past and promising future. This is the chronicle of our 8-day odyssey, a testament to the transformative power of travel and the boundless horizons that await those who dare to explore.

Contents

Embarking on an Enriching Journey through Vietnam (October 15th to 22nd, 2018)	2
~:Day 1:~ Tour of Ho Chi Minh City (The second capital of Vietnam, earlier known as Saigon)	7
~:Day 2:~ Exploring the Enchanting Mekong Delta: A Journey of Discovery	27
~:Day 3:~ On the Way to Hoi An - Where Tranquillity meets Adventure.	44
~:Day 4:~ Tour of the Golden Bridge and Ba Na Hills	48
~:Day 5:~ Hanoi Unveiled : A Day of Heritage and Flavour	58
~:Day 6:~ Tour of Ha Long Bay	62
~:Day 7:~ Returns back to Hanoi	69
~:Day 8:~ Return journey to Kolkata	77
Epilogue	81
About the Author	*103*

"The basic core of a man's living spirit is his passion for adventure. The joy of life comes from our encounters with new experiences, and hence there is no greater joy than to have an endlessly changing horizon, for each day to have a new and different sun."

— Christopher McCandless

Embarking on an Enriching Journey through Vietnam (October 15th to 22nd, 2018)

The decision to visit Vietnam during October 2018, from the 15th to the 22nd, proved to be a truly enriching experience. Many questioned my choice of destination, prompting me to clarify my reasons. There were two primary motivations behind my decision.

Firstly, I made a friend, Ms Phi, an educator and actress in Vietnamese shows and series, from Vietnam through a social networking site, and our interactions unveiled Vietnam's exceptional beauty—both in its historical significance and as a tourist destination. Secondly, I couldn't help but notice the striking parallels between my homeland, India, and Vietnam. Both nations had endured foreign rule and colonisation, both had been scarred by war and devastation, and both continue to strive for progress and prosperity. However, my visit to Vietnam would soon reveal the subtle yet significant differences between our two nations, which I'll delve into shortly.

Let's embark on this journey of happiness, as we meticulously plan to explore four key tourist destinations within Vietnam: Ho Chi Minh City, Hoi

An, Ha Long Bay, and Hanoi. It's worth noting that there are no direct flights from India to Vietnam, so our adventure began with a flight from Kolkata to Ho Chi Minh City via Bangkok. Our departure from Kolkata was scheduled for 1:45 am according to Indian Standard Time. It's important to mention that Vietnam is 1 and ½ hours ahead of Indian time. Vietnam shares the same time zone throughout the country, which is also known as Indochina Time. After a journey of approximately 6 and ½ hours, including a 1-hour layover in Bangkok, we touched down at Tan Son Nhat International Airport, HCMC at 10:17 am local time.

Ho Chi Minh City, situated in South Vietnam, is the country's second-largest city, it bears a striking resemblance to Kolkata, as the Saigon River flows through the city, much like the Ganges flows through Kolkata. The city was historically known as Saigon but was renamed after the Vietnam War in honour of Ho Chi Minh, a revered revolutionary and freedom fighter in Vietnam's history. Ho Chi Minh played a pivotal role in the war against the USA and the reunification of North Vietnam and South Vietnam.

What I learned about Vietnam after visiting and meeting people there, and from the Internet is that Vietnam is home to a diverse and vibrant population with a rich cultural heritage shaped by centuries of history, traditions, and influences. Here are some key aspects of the people of Vietnam I would like to share in my book:

Ethnicity: The majority of the population in Vietnam is of the Kinh ethnicity, also known as the Viet people, who constitute about 85% of the total population. However, Vietnam is also home to a mosaic of ethnic minority groups, each with its own distinct traditions, languages, and customs. Some of the prominent ethnic minorities include the Tay, Thai, Muong, Hmong, and Khmer people.

Language: The official language of Vietnam is Vietnamese (Tiếng Việt), which is part of the Austroasiatic language family. It uses Latin script with diacritics for tones. Ethnic minority groups often speak their own languages, contributing to the linguistic diversity of the country.

Religion: Buddhism is the predominant religion in Vietnam, with a significant number of followers adhering to Mahayana Buddhism. Other religions practised include Taoism, Confucianism, Christianity (Catholicism and Protestantism), and indigenous beliefs and traditions.

Family and Society: Vietnamese society places a strong emphasis on family values and filial piety. Respect for elders and ancestors is deeply ingrained, and families often live in multigenerational households. Traditional gender roles are still prevalent in many aspects of society, although modernization and urbanization have brought about changes in social dynamics.

Cuisine: Vietnamese cuisine is renowned for its freshness, the balance of flavours, and the use of aromatic herbs and spices. Staples include rice, noodles, seafood, pork, and a variety of vegetables. Dishes like pho (noodle soup), banh mi (Vietnamese sandwich), and spring rolls have gained international acclaim.

Art and Culture: Vietnam boasts a rich cultural heritage expressed through art forms such as traditional music (including the distinctive đàn bầu or monochord instrument), dance (like the graceful ao dai dance), water puppetry, and intricate handicrafts such as lacquerware, silk embroidery, and pottery.

Education: Education is highly valued in Vietnamese society, and there is a strong emphasis on academic achievement. Literacy rates are relatively high, and the country has made significant strides in expanding access to education at all levels.

Economic Activities: Vietnam's economy is diverse, with agriculture, manufacturing, services, and tourism playing significant roles. Agriculture remains important, with rice cultivation being a staple, while industries such as textiles, electronics, and tourism have seen rapid growth in recent years.

Overall, the people of Vietnam are known for their resilience, hospitality, and strong cultural identity, making them an integral part of the country's vibrant tapestry.

"Travelling leaves you speechless, turns you into a storyteller."

— Ibn Battuta

~:Day 1:~ Tour of Ho Chi Minh City (The second capital of Vietnam, earlier known as Saigon)

We stayed at Eden Garden Hotel, 28/12 Bui Vien, Pham Ngu Lao Ward, District 1, Ho Chi Minh City

The first thing that came to my notice was despite the large population of the city, in comparison to their country, the common people maintained high ethical values like cleanliness and were humble to the visitors. The hotel that we booked is a place very similar to the Esplanade of Kolkata, but the place is cleaner and more organised. There are a lot of places, memorials, museums, temples, and pagodas to visit within the city.

From the HCMC International Airport, we move on to Eden Garden Hotel, 28/12 Bui Vien, Pham Ngu Lao Ward, District 1, Ho Chi Minh City. As I had booked a guided tour of the city, on arrival at the Eden Garden Hotel, our guide was already waiting for us. We refreshed ourselves and after having a heavy breakfast in a nearby Indian restaurant with Aalu Paratha, Tomato sauce, Curd and salad, we went on to the city tour. We boarded the car and moved on to explore the city named after the great leader, Ho Chi Minh.

As the sun began to cast its golden rays upon the vibrant streets of Ho Chi Minh City, our day of exploration and adventure was set to begin. We enlisted the services of a knowledgeable local guide and hopped into a comfortable cab, ready to embark on a city tour that promised to be both enriching and captivating. Our first stop was the War Remnants Museum, a poignant reminder of Vietnam's tumultuous past. Walking through the exhibits, I was transported back in time to the Vietnam War era. The haunting images, artefacts, and stories of resilience left a deep impression on me. It was a sombre yet essential start to the day, reminding me of the importance of peace and diplomacy.

Discovering Vietnam's Historical Heritage: The War Remnants Museum

Location: 28 Duong Le Quy Don Phuong
Located in the heart of District 3, in Ho Chi Minh City, the War Remnants Museum is a symbol of Vietnam's past. Run by the Ho Chi Minh City government this museum provides an understanding of the events related to the First Indochina War and the Vietnam War through its array of displays.

The museum's history dates back to September 4 1975 when it was established as the Exhibition House for US and Puppet Crimes. This original name reflects the charged atmosphere in war Vietnam characterized by strong animosity towards the United States and its allies. Over time the museum underwent name changes to mirror shifts in Vietnam's climate and global relations.

In 1990 it was rebranded as the Museum of Chinese and American War Crimes to denounce war atrocities on a scale beyond U.S. Involvement. However, a significant transformation took place in 1995 with improved relations between Vietnam and the United States and the lifting of U.S. Sanctions. It was, during this time that the museum adopted its name, the War Remnants Museum.

The decision to rename the museum signalled a shift, towards an approach recognizing the complexities of history while also promoting healing and understanding.

Upon entering the War Remnants Museum visitors are greeted with a story that transcends boundaries and beliefs. The curated galleries offer a look at how the wars impacted Vietnam and its people. Through photographs, artefacts, personal accounts and testimonies the museum provides a moving. Sometimes disturbing exploration of events.

A key focus of the museum is to highlight the toll of the Vietnam War showcasing the suffering endured by both civilians and soldiers. The exhibits emphasize the effects of chemical warfare particularly highlighting the impact of Agent Orange on generations of individuals. By presenting photographs, documents and personal stories visitors can grasp firsthand how the war has left effects on health and nature.

Another significant aspect of the museum's collection is its depiction of war propaganda and how media influenced perception during wartime. Visitors have an opportunity to examine propaganda materials from perspectives involved in the conflict offering insights into information dissemination and manipulation during that era.

Furthermore, The War Remnants Museum reveals insights into war movements and Vietnam's solidarity, with other nations striving for independence and peace.

Exhibits, at the museum honour the efforts of activists and groups who supported Vietnam's cause and advocated for an end to the war.

As guests explore the museum's displays they are confronted with the realities of war. Also witness moments of strength, bravery and optimism. The museum's main message revolves around remembering and reconciling urging visitors to ponder the past while embracing a future rooted in understanding and collaboration.

In summary, the War Remnants Museum stands as a solemn yet crucial symbol of Vietnam's history. Its transformation from a symbol of war anger to a beacon of reconciliation mirrors Vietnam's own path toward healing and progress. By engaging with its exhibits and absorbing its narratives visitors develop an understanding of the complexities of war and the resilience of nature.

Our hearts were deeply moved following our visit to the War museum by the photo gallery depicting victims including women and children affected by the war aftermath.

Our next stop was Chinatown, a district that showcases Ho Chi Minh City's cultural heritage. The vibrant colours of shophouses and delightful scents, from street food vendors transported me to another world.

We wandered down the quaint streets pausing to enjoy cuisine and browsing the lively markets.

Exploring Cho Lon – Saigon's Bustling China Town

Location: District 5, Ho Chi Minh City

Nestled in the fabric of Ho Chi Minh City is Cho Lon, affectionately referred to as Saigon's China Town. This bustling area, known as the " market " invites visitors from, over the world to soak in its vibrant atmosphere and rich cultural history.

At the core of Cho Lon lies the energetic Binh Tay Market, a sprawling marketplace that embodies the district's spirit. Located on Tran Hung Dao Boulevard along the west bank of the Saigon River Cho Lon has become a must-visit spot for those exploring the city.

The charm of Cho Lon goes beyond its streets and bustling markets; it has also captivated enthusiasts. Marguerite Duras's autobiographical novel "The Lover" (1984) immortalizes Cho Lon as the setting for a love story adding a layer of allure to this already fascinating location.

During the day Cho Lon buzzes with activity as traders and shoppers engage in exchanges at Binh Tay Market. This essential part of the district offers a range of products from delicacies to traditional handicrafts. For food lovers renowned restaurants like Aquatria, Dong Khanh and Bat Dat entice, with mouthwatering flavours that represent Saigon's landscape.

As night descends Cho Lon undergoes a captivating change. The glow of neon lights brightens up the streets painting a picture, across the district. Visitors come in droves to enjoy Hoa cuisine savouring dishes like dumplings Duong Chau fried rice and Tu Xuyen tofu in the evening ambience.

Weekends are bustling in Cho Lon with locals bustling around for festivities and tourists soaking in the vibes. On the other hand, weekdays offer a serene charm for those looking to leisurely explore the district.

A trip to Thien Hau Temple is a highlight of Cho Lon providing insights into the heritage of the area. Many tours of Ho Chi Minh City include Cho Lon on their routes allowing travellers to delve into Saigon's tapestry.

On our group excursion, we uncovered treasures nestled in Cho Lon's busy streets. Tasting versions of pho and other local delicacies added a flavour to our journey turning it into an unforgettable culinary experience.

Navigating through Cho Lon's streets can be both exhilarating and overwhelming; thus having a knowledgeable guide, by your side is priceless. They can lead you through markets ensuring you get the most out of your exploration and cultural immersion.

As night falls and the lights of Cho Lon begin to glow the district's charm truly comes alive. Join us on this adventure, where the rich cultural blend of Saigon unfolds in the bustling streets and lively markets of Cho Lon. Step into the enchanting world of Cho Lon – a chapter, in Ho Chi Minh City's captivating tale.

Our exploration led us to the Binh Tay Market, where I found myself surrounded by an array of colours, exotic fruits and handmade crafts. Haggling with vendors for souvenirs was an experience to remember. I departed with a bag of treasures and a newfound admiration, for the city's market scene.

Binh Tay Market – A vibrant Hub in Saigon's Chinatown

Location: 57A Thap Muoi, Ward 2, District 6

In the heart of Ho Chi Minh City lies Binh Tay Market, a part of Cho Lon, also known as Saigon's Chinatown. This lively market town, in District 6 provides an array of experiences for travellers to soak up its atmosphere and cultural offerings.

To get to Binh Tay Market from the Independence Palace take a route along Nam Ky Khoi Nghia Street and then turn onto Vo Van Kiet Street. A right turn onto Ngo Nhan Tinh Street will lead you to Phan Van Khoe Street, where you'll catch sight of the market's energy on the side.

Binh Tay Market is open from 7 am to 6 pm turning into a hub where both sellers and buyers are engulfed in its ambiance. The market's distinctive bagua shape and spacious design create a setting that invites exploration. Its architectural allure, blending aesthetics with techniques is apparent in the central tower flanked by synchronized clock symbols and intricately crafted tiled roofs.

With 12 gates inside Binh Tay Market and a grand entrance facing Cho Lon bus station, 2,300 stalls offer an array of products catering to various preferences – from household items and spices to fashion accessories and jewellery. The lower level of the market is filled with an assortment of products, like kitchenware, spices, textiles and household goods while the upper floor displays a collection of ready-to-wear clothing and sweet treats.

Exploring the sections of the market will introduce you to Tran Binh's top-notch spices and seafood Le Tan Kes diverse food items and Phan Van Khoe's lively food selling area. Make sure to try out the dishes offered at stalls serving traditional favourites such as porridge, bamboo shoots and vermicelli noodles that create a delightful mix of flavours.

One of the standout culinary delights at this market is Pha Lau known for its broth and tantalizing aromas along with Bun Rieu cherished for its vermicelli noodles prepared from secret recipes passed down through generations.

Visiting Binh Tay Market offers an experience; however, it's important to be aware that most vendors primarily sell in bulk or bundles. Haggling skills can be beneficial in securing quality goods at prices. Navigating through the market streets can be exciting; therefore, having an experienced guide, with you can enhance your visit. While strolling through the lanes of Binh Tay Market and enjoying its food offerings you'll discover the lively spirit of Cho Lon and the enchanting allure of Saigon's Chinatown. Immerse yourself in the culture savour flavours and soak in the vibrant atmosphere of this iconic market hub.

Our final morning destination was the Thien Hau Temple, a sanctuary, amidst the busy streets. The detailed architecture and the aroma of burning incense set a calming mood. I paused to contemplate and show my reverence before embarking on our afternoon escapades.

Thien Hau Pagoda – A Tranquil Oasis in the Heart of Ho Chi Minh City

Location: 705 Đuong Nguyen Trai, Phuong 11, District 5

Nestled within the cityscape of Ho Chi Minh City, the Thien Hau Pagoda stands as a haven that attracts travellers from around the world seeking spiritual solace. This sacred sanctuary, cherished by both locals and tourists showcases the gems of this destination providing a calm escape from the city's hectic pace.

Approaching the Thien Hau Pagoda visitors are captivated by its feature—the unique pendant hanging above. This special tradition encourages guests to write their wishes or prayers on paper rings, which are then hung alongside incense sticks as offerings to Mrs. Thien Hau adding a touch to the journey. This practice highlights the importance of the temple in the lives of Saigon's community reflected in every aspect brought over from China including precious woods and intricate figurines.

Situated on bustling Nguyen Trai Street, the temple greets you with an iron gate that leads to a charming courtyard. Delicate porcelain statues embellish the roof, with symbols and tales while wooden replicas of Chinese theatres and lanterns contribute to the tranquil atmosphere.

Upon entering the courtyard partially covered unveils an altar honouring Mazu, the Goddess of the Sea.

Incense holders are scattered throughout the areas welcoming guests to take part in standing customs.

The temple's rooftop is decorated with captivating porcelain scenes depicting moments from a century town featuring a diverse cast of characters and historical tales ranging from Taoist Immortal Sages to legendary warriors such, as Guan Yu.

At the centre of Thien Hau Pagoda, three bronze statues of the Goddess demand attention, their clothing and peaceful expressions infusing an element into the shrine. The lingering fragrance of burning incense permeates the surroundings heightening the atmosphere of tranquillity and calm that envelops this site offering a setting for introspection and spiritual connection.

For shutterbugs, Thien Hau Pagoda serves as a feast for the eyes with its elements and deep cultural significance serving as a captivating focal point. The temple's genuine allure, from its crafted interiors to its courtyard beckons visitors to capture its essence through photography preserving enduring memories of this profound spiritual voyage.

When exploring Vietnam, a stop at Thien Hau Pagoda is essential, for gaining insight into the nation's legacy and architectural grandeur. Immerse yourself in the temple's charm and deep tranquillity leaving you with recollections of an immensely rewarding journey that transcends both time and location. In the afternoon we arrived at the Independence Palace also referred to as the Reunification Palace. Walking through this landmark was, like taking a trip to the 1970s. The maintained rooms and artefacts provided me with insight into Vietnam's past. The extensive gardens and majestic palace stood out against our visit, to the war museum showcasing the country's strength and advancement.

Independence Palace – Witness to Vietnam's Historic Transformations

Location: 135 Nam Ky Khoi Nghia Street, Ben Nghe Ward, District 1

Located in the heart of Ho Chi Minh City, the Independence Palace also known as Reunification Palace stands proudly as a cherished landmark that embodies Vietnam's turbulent past. Situated at 135 Nam Ky Khoi Nghia Street Ben Nghe Ward, District 1 this iconic structure serves not as an entity but, as a vivid portrayal of Vietnam's history beckoning travellers to delve into its cultural legacy.

Upon approaching the palace one is captivated by its splendour crafted by Ngô Viết Thụ that beautifully captures the essence of traditions. Acting as both a residence and an administrative center for the President of the Republic of Vietnam it holds significance as a symbol of governance during moments in Vietnamese history.

Visitors are welcome to explore the palace between 07:30 AM to 11:30 AM and from 1 PM to 5 PM to immerse themselves in its narrative. Admission prices stand at 40,000 VND for adults 20,000 VND for students and 10,000 VND for children; additional charges may apply for access to areas or exhibitions.

The palace's profound historical relevance is highlighted by the events of April 30th, 1975 when a tank, from the North Vietnamese Army breached its gates during the Fall of Saigon. An event that signified the conclusion of the Vietnam War.

This significant moment, forever ingrained in history led to the palace being a Reunification Hall by the Provisional Revolutionary Government symbolizing the unity of the country under a government.

Exploring the Independence Palace isn't just a tour; it's a journey, in time that offers travellers and history enthusiasts a chance to witness Vietnam's resilience and transformation. The walls echo with memories of events beckoning visitors to honour the nation's past and discover Vietnam's cultural tapestry. It serves as a tribute to the spirit of the people making it a must-visit for those interested in uncovering the nation's intricate history and vibrant heritage.

During our visit, to Ho Chi Minh City we encountered traces of its colonial past at Notre Dame Cathedral and the Old Central Post Office. The cathedral's exterior and exquisite interiors left me spellbound. The post office's architectural charm and the nostalgic act of sending postcards created lasting memories that will stay with me for years to come.

Notre Dame Cathedral – A Symbol of Faith and History

Location: 01 Cong Xa Paris, Ben Nghe Ward, District 1

The Notre Dame Cathedral, a symbol of faith and history stands proudly in downtown Ho Chi Minh City, Vietnam. Known as Nhà Thờ Đức Bà, in Vietnamese this stunning architectural wonder attracts travellers interested in exploring Christian heritage and cultural significance. Built between 1863 and 1880 the cathedral boasts mesmerizing architecture. Its impressive frontage and tall spires showcase a blend of Gothic and Romanesque styles that captivate visitors with its grandeur. Strolling around Notre Dame Cathedral allows you to soak in the atmosphere of Saigon. The beautiful 30/4 Park located in front of the cathedral provides a tranquil setting for reflection. Adjacent to it the Saigon Central Post Office and modern business hubs blend charm with energy.

A leisurely stroll from Ben Thanh Market to the cathedral offers a glimpse into Saigon's character from towering skyscrapers to edifices. If you're fortunate you may witness a group of doves taking flight enhancing the cathedral ambience. For those interested, in an experience attending an English Mass at the cathedral every Sunday at 9:30 AM presents an opportunity to engage with the local Christian community in worship within this iconic location.

Discovering the Notre Dame Cathedral area reveals a hub of activity. Begin your exploration at 30/4 Park. Enjoy a cup of " coffee " a local favourite in the serene surroundings of the park. Diamond Plaza offers a variety of shopping options while cafes, like Trung Nguyen and Highland, provide a setting to relax and take in the city views. When it comes to dining the vicinity around Notre Dame Cathedral presents an array of delights. Ghem serves rice dishes and coffee while Ong Tam specializes in Saigon cuisine. For a hotpot experience visit Lau Cong Chua on the floor of Diamond Plaza.

A trip to Notre Dame Cathedral goes beyond sightseeing; it's an immersion, into Saigon's culture, history and spiritual legacy. It's a place where the past blends seamlessly with the present inviting visitors to embrace both the serenity of faith and the dynamic energy of the city.

Traveller's Guide to the Old Central Post Office

Location: 2 Cong Xa Paris, Ben Nghe, District 1

Walking through the doors of the Old Central Post Office, in Ho Chi Minh City feels like taking a journey in time to Vietnam period. This impressive structure, situated in District 1 stands proudly as a symbol of the country's history and stunning architecture. Designed by Gustave Eiffel, the mastermind behind Paris's iconic Eiffel Tower this historic building was constructed between 1886 and 1891 during the colonial era. Beyond its function as a post office, it holds cultural importance that every visitor should experience.

The intricate Gothic and Renaissance architectural elements of the building immediately draw your gaze as you approach it. The towering vaulted roof, delicate ironwork details and gracefully arched windows create a captivating sight that hints at the grandeur. Stepping into the interior reveals a hall adorned with beautifully painted maps showcasing Saigon, Cholon and nearby areas. These maps do not provide a glimpse into the past. Also, double as exquisite works of art.

A delightful nod to history is found in the phone booths dating back to the 20th century – a charming reminder of communication methods, from days gone by.

Many visitors are drawn to the portrait of Ho Chi Minh, a figure, in modern Vietnam, which adds a sense of respect to the atmosphere and serves as a popular spot for photos.

Take a moment to admire the details found throughout the building from the wooden shutters to the decorative designs that transport you back in time. Despite its history, the Old Central Post Office continues to function as a post office allowing guests to buy stamps, postcards and even mail letters from this iconic setting. It's an experience to engage in the timeless custom of sending mail while surrounded by historical significance.

Within the premises, various shops and stalls offer souvenirs, local handicrafts and postcards making it an ideal place to discover mementoes or gifts to remember your visit. Visitors should be aware that the Old Central Post Office is open daily from 7:00 AM to 7:00 PM; visiting in the morning is advisable to avoid crowds. While entry into the hall is free there might be a charge, for accessing certain areas or exploring the mezzanine level.

Whether you have an interest, in architecture a love for history or are simply a traveller, a trip to the Old Central Post Office offers a glimpse into Vietnam's colonial past and takes you on a nostalgic journey through time. This iconic building is sure to leave you with memories and a newfound respect for the cultural heritage of the country.

Upon our return from exploring the city during the day, we decided to take some time to relax at our hotel before heading out for an evening stroll at the sunset. The moon began its ascent. Our destination this time was none, other than Ben Thanh Market, an embodiment of Saigon's essence.

Ben Thanh Market – A Century of Saigon's Spirit

Location: Le Loi, Ben Thanh Ward, District 1

As the sun started to dip below the horizon, in Ho Chi Minh City, my spouse and I found ourselves fully engrossed in the vibe of Ben Thanh Market. The bustling chatter of vendors showcasing their goods the tempting scents wafting from street food stalls and the vibrant array of products on offer all contributed to an experience that we were keen to delve into.

We leisurely wandered through the market's four entrances, each revealing its collection of items. The southern entrance caught our attention with its dazzling selection of clothes, fabrics and jewellery. My wife was captivated by the patterns on Vietnamese outfits known as Ao Dai while I admired the skilful workmanship displayed in handmade jewellery pieces. Heading towards the entrance we were welcomed by the mouthwatering aroma of prepared Vietnamese delicacies. We savoured a bowl of steaming pho, a noodle soup that is a beloved part of Vietnamese culinary tradition. The lively buzz created by locals and visitors added to the market atmosphere.

As darkness enveloped Ben Thanh Market it underwent a captivating transformation. Illuminated stalls lit up the pathways casting a glow, over our nighttime exploration. We stumbled upon an antique store nestled in a corner its shelves adorned with distinctive treasures reflecting Vietnam's diverse heritage.

During our visit, to Ben Thanh Market we were drawn to a carved figurine portraying a traditional Vietnamese scene. The shop owner shared captivating tales about its origins and the intricate craftsmanship behind it making it a special keepsake from our time. Exploring the night market further, we stumbled upon hidden treasures at every corner. From handcrafted ceramics to textiles and local artwork each piece reflects Vietnam's cultural tapestry. Unable to resist we acquired a set of teacups as a memento of our magical evening in Saigon.

As we said goodbye to Ben Thanh Market memories filled our hearts and our bags were brimming with finds. The market's timeless allure, vibrant atmosphere and diverse offerings left an impression on our exploration of Ho Chi Minh City's core. Our culinary adventure continued with a dinner at a Vietnamese eatery where the flavours of Vietnam delighted our palates once more surrounded by the warmth of good company.

Retreating to our lodgings at the end of the day, in the Mekong Delta we carried with us cherished memories and enriching experiences.

It was a day filled with adventure learning about the culture and savouring food—a memorable experience exploring the stunning landscapes and rich history of Vietnam.

"Wherever you go becomes a part of you somehow."

— Anita Desai

~:Day 2:~ Exploring the Enchanting Mekong Delta: A Journey of Discovery

The day we set off on an exhilarating journey, to the Mekong Delta situated to the south of Ho Chi Minh City. Our exploration took us through a maze of canals, fields, fruit orchards and delightful villages that define this charming region. Our group comprised 12 individuals from parts of the world. Spain, Italy, the USA, Indonesia and us from India. Our tour guide, a woman though not fluent in English shared information with us confidently.

Visiting the Mekong Delta had always been an aspiration, for us. On the day of our excursion my wife and I began our Classic Mekong Delta Tour filled with anticipation and excitement.

The tour we signed up for promised a day of immersing ourselves in the culture taking in the beauty of nature and savouring delicious food – and we were thrilled at the prospect of experiencing it all. Our adventure kicked off with a pickup, from our hotel in Ho Chi Minh City, where we were warmly welcomed by our guide and fellow travellers. The journey to the Mekong Delta was a delight with views of countryside and expansive rice fields that seemed to stretch on endlessly. Vietnam's renowned rice bowl truly lived up to its reputation.

However, our day got off to a bit of a start due to a mix-up. The tour was set to begin at 8 a.m. Time. I mistakenly set my alarm based on Indian time causing us to be delayed by an hour and a half. As a result, we only woke up at 8 a.m. making us late for the tour departure. Thankfully our fellow travellers were understanding. After apologizing to everyone we managed to board the bus at 8:48 a.m. To catch up on lost time we had to skip the breakfast at the hotel. Instead, we had an opportunity to enjoy breakfast at a roadside café along the way – complete with spots perfect for capturing some beautiful photographs.

Our first stop was a welcome, at the Mekong Rest Stop.

We took a stroll savoured some drinks and readied ourselves for the upcoming adventure along, picking up a few local treasures like handmade crafts and cultural artefacts that beautifully represented Vietnam's rich heritage.

Upon arrival at the Mekong River, we hopped on a ferry that carried us to the heart of the delta area. The river like the Ganges flowed with its waters and was adorned with floating homes of indigenous fishermen. It served as a mode of transport in that locality. Two distinct islands stood out in the river. We disembarked onto one of them. Venturing further into the island we engaged with the local tasted fruits and tea enjoyed their music and songs and captured precious moments through photography.

Afterward, we embarked on a boat for a cruise, along the canals of the delta region. The tranquil waters mirrored greenery under blue skies above—a picturesque sight indeed. Drifting through these canals allowed us to witness firsthand the way of life unfolding before our eyes; villagers going about their routine children playing near the water's edge and fishermen skilfully casting their nets.

One of the parts of the cruise was when we visited local workshops where they made coconut candy and crispy rice cakes. We were truly amazed watching skilled artisans showcase their talents. We even got to taste some of the treats they created. The friendly vendors shared stories, about life in the Mekong Delta, which helped us understand and respect their culture and traditions.

On our journey through the canals of the Mekong Delta, my wife and I had the pleasure of meeting two families whose stories have stayed with us sparking discussions about joy and independence.

One family was from Malaysia consisting of a mother and her daughter along with her daughter-in-law. All three women. What was exceptional, about their trip was that they left their homes and children in their husbands' care for two months as they explored East Asia. They travelled through bustling streets in Vietnam and experienced Japan's charm, soaked in

South Korea's wealth before heading home. It wasn't a test of their husband's abilities to handle household duties and childcare. Also showcased the strong trust and support within their family.

We wished them health and a strong bond of love and togetherness that lasts forever.

The second family, from the United States, consisted of a couple with the husband's parents. Their journey took them through Europe and Asia for three months including a stop in Vietnam. After exploring Indonesia, they were now embracing the culture of Vietnam and planning visits to Thailand and Dubai before returning to the US. In our discussions, I invited them to discover the sights of India such as the Taj Mahal, the serene Himalayas, the sunny beaches of Goa, the peaceful backwaters of Kerala rugged mountains of Ladakh, historic forts in Rajasthan, the fertile Gangetic plains, the mystical Sundarbans and charming hill station Darjeeling. We also shared insights, about India's cuisine and intricate crafts before time constraints brought our conversation to an end. They kindly extended an invitation for us to visit the US too fostering a sense of friendship and mutual exploration.

Our travels also took us to the views of Ba Na Hills, where we unexpectedly met the family from the United States highlighting the magic of chance encounters and shared moments, in the world of travel.

Continuing our journey a stroll through an orchard allowed us to sample a variety of seasonal fruits while being serenaded by traditional music in the background. The flavours of the fruits were truly delightful. We relished each bite as we listened to the melodies. A visit to a Honey Bee farm was another highlight. We learned about honey production processes. Got to taste a hot tea made from the farm's honey. It was a distinct beverage that we thoroughly enjoyed.

Our next escapade involved boarding boats where five individuals, including the boatman, could sit in a single row. This part of our journey was admittedly slightly nerve-wracking as none of us were proficient swimmers and the canal we traversed was deep, narrow and bustling with boat traffic. Eventually, we reached our destination in the heart of the Mekong Delta where we relished cuisine for lunch. Dining, at a garden restaurant overlooking the Mekong Delta River bank made lunchtime more special. The rural landscape was stunning. The local delicacies we enjoyed were a delight, for all the senses.

Our lunch on the captivating Mekong River journey was truly a masterpiece, a feast that delighted our taste buds and made a lasting impression on our food adventure. Surrounded by greenery and peaceful river scenery our group of twelve a mix of different backgrounds and cultures gathered to savour an unforgettable dining experience. The selected menu showcased the flavours of Vietnamese cuisine with an array of dishes that captured the essence of the region. We kicked off with a comforting Vegetable Soup filled with herbs and vegetables setting the tone for what was ahead.

Then came the highlights – juicy BBQ Chicken and BBQ Fish grilled to perfection each bite packed with flavours and aromatic spices. The crispy Spring Rolls filled with vegetables added a texture to our meal. The Vietnamese specialty Pancakes (Banh Xeo) stole the spotlight with their crispiness and flavourful filling creating a blend of textures and tastes. The colourful Mixed Vegetables brought freshness to our plates adding a touch, to our dining experience.

Savouring the combination of Steamed Rice, with rich sauces and flavours elevated our lunch experience to a new level of satisfaction. A delightful Fruit Dessert served as the finale, blending flavours harmoniously to wrap up our lavish meal. Amidst laughter and lively conversations, our lunch transformed into a memory symbolizing unity through the shared joy of food that transcends divides.

Following lunch, we had a choice to make; some in our group opted for a bicycle ride while others, including us decided to explore on foot through fruit gardens and fields. Upon reaching our meeting point we rejoined our bus for the return journey to Ho Chi Minh City.

Before heading to HCMC we visited the Vinh Trang Pagoda—a fusion of Vietnamese, Chinese and

Cambodian architectural styles. The intricate design details of the pagoda left us in awe as we wandered through its surroundings and absorbed its significance. As we journeyed back to Ho Chi Minh City we reminisced about the day's adventures, with memories. The experience we had on the Classic Mekong Delta Tour went beyond what we had hoped for. It provided us with an insight, into the culture and stunning natural landscapes of this captivating area. It was a day that will stay with us for a time standing out as a highlight of our travels abroad leaving us with cherished memories and a newfound admiration for Vietnam's beauty.

As we made our way back to the city the moment of goodbyes slowly approached. The first to bid farewell was the family from the United States, their warm smiles and heartfelt farewells signalling the beginning of our departure. Amidst lingering on the bus savouring those shared moments of our journey an atmosphere of gratitude filled the air. It was a time to express our appreciation to the organizers who meticulously planned every aspect of our trip. A special mention was given to our guide whose constant presence and informative explanations enhanced every part of our experiences.

From understanding traditions, to navigating markets our guide offered unwavering support ensuring that our journey went beyond mere sightseeing to truly immerse ourselves in the essence of the region. Their knowledge went beyond handling logistics, including suggestions, for local cuisine help with finding mementoes and engaging stories about the historical and cultural importance of every place we explored. With gratitude and cherished memories, we said goodbye to our hosts thankful for their commitment and warmth that turned our adventure, in the Mekong Delta into a part of our travel story.

Evening Walk and Dining

After we returned from our trip to the Mekong Delta, my spouse and I decided to take a short break at the hotel. The peaceful moments we spent there allowed us to reflect on the depth of our experiences. Little did we anticipate that our quiet time would be interrupted by a surprise.

Ms. Phi, a friend from my circle kindly made her way to our hotel to meet us. The attentive hotel manager promptly notified us of her arrival. Ensured her comfort in the waiting area until we could gather together. Excitedly we headed to the lounge where we were met with her welcoming smile. Ms. Phi, fresh from a day's work exuded a sense of familiarity and friendship.

Despite facing language barriers that made communication challenging our clever hotel manager volunteered as a translator bridging the gap between languages and enabling our conversation to flow smoothly. Our encounter became more meaningful as we exchanged gifts representing the essence of our cultures. From colourful Batik print cotton clothing from Shantiniketan to a 5-inch brass Buddha idol we offered Ms. Phi mementoes symbolizing our journey, from India. We enjoyed an array of sweets and snacks, from Kolkata, savouring the flavours of our homeland.

Laughter and joy filled the air as we indulged in the treats sharing conversations despite the language barrier. The universal language of hospitality and friendship resonated deeply. Though Ms. Phi kindly invited us to her home our packed schedule led us to decline. Bid farewell to Ms. Phi, who left with a heart of happiness we continued with our plans, cherishing memories of an evening with new friends at Eden Garden Hotel.

As the sun set we wrapped up our day with two experiences; a Water Puppetry show and a special dinner at a floating restaurant. Water puppetry is a part of Vietnam's Cultural Heritage. A living depiction of its history and culture. Watching this art form offered us insights, into life and traditions.

Traveller's Guide to Water Puppetry Show

Location: 55B Nguyen Thi Minh Khai, Ben Thanh Ward, District 1

As the sun set below the skyline painting a hue, over the busy streets of Ho Chi Minh City I felt my excitement mounting for the cultural journey ahead; the Water Puppetry Show. Situated in the heart of this city the show seemed to offer a one-of-a-kind and captivating experience that merged tradition, artistry and entertainment in a manner unique to Vietnamese culture.

The setting for this show was none other than the Golden Dragon Water Puppet Theater, a name that conjured images of ancient stories and mystical displays. As my spouse and I strolled towards the theater we were welcomed by the tunes of Vietnamese music wafting through the air setting a tone of eagerness and curiosity. Upon entering the theater we were immediately struck by its ambiance. The traditional Vietnamese architectural details, adorned with carvings and tasteful decorations further added to the allure of our evening. The venue buzzed with conversation, from audience members – locals and visitors alike – all eagerly anticipating this timeless art form brought to life.

With lights dimmed and curtains drawn back, we found ourselves whisked away into a realm of awe-inspiring magic and fascination.

The shimmering water, on the stage sparkled softly under the glow of the stage lights setting the scene for the puppet to make its appearance. It moved gracefully across the water's surface as if guided by magic. The performance continued with a series of scenes each portraying aspects of Vietnamese folklore, mythology and everyday life. From moments of village children chasing butterflies to battles between legendary heroes and mythical beings, the puppetry was expertly crafted, captivating our imaginations and immersing us in the stories being portrayed.

One of the parts of the show was a traditional dragon dance featuring a magnificent dragon puppet emerging from beneath the water's depths its vibrant scales shining under the spotlight. The intricate movements of the dragon skilfully manipulated by puppeteers backstage brought this creature to life in a mesmerizing and enchanting manner. Throughout the performance, live music provided a backdrop adding layers of emotion and depth to the puppetry on display. The melodies of instruments like đàn bầu and bamboo flutes filled the auditorium whisking us away into Vietnam's heritage. As the final scenes played out and the last puppet vanished beneath the water's surface thunderous applause erupted from the audience marking an end, to an evening.

My spouse. I whispered excitedly to each other reminiscing about our moments, from the show and admiring the skill and imagination of the puppeteers.

As we left the theater we carried not memories of an enthralling performance but a deeper respect for Vietnamese culture and the timeless beauty of water puppetry. The Water Puppetry Show in Ho Chi Minh City was truly a highlight of our journey a treasure that touched our hearts and minds. Witnessing the art of water puppetry in Ho Chi Minh City is a cultural experience that leaves travellers captivated. Originating from the century this traditional Vietnamese art has transformed into a captivating display that celebrates the nation's rich heritage and legends. Here is your go-to guide for exploring the realm of water puppetry during your trip, to Ho Chi Minh City.

Here is some more information, about the Puppetry shows in Ho Chi Minh City:

Location and Venue: The Golden Dragon Water Puppet Theater is a hub for this art form in HCMC situated at 55B Nguyen Thi Minh Khai, Ben Thanh Ward, District 1. This known spot sets the stage for a water puppetry experience, blending artistry, music and storytelling in a unique theatrical presentation.

Show Highlights: Water puppetry is a captivating display that takes place on a water stage featuring crafted puppets dancing to the beat of traditional music. The colourful puppets, meticulously designed come to life against the backdrop of a tranquil water surface. Although the narrative is presented in Vietnamese the stories go beyond language barriers by conveying tales of life, legends and myths through puppet movements and gestures. Upon entering the theater you can expect to be welcomed by an atmosphere filled with excitement. The show typically lasts from 45 minutes to an hour, during which one will witness the following:

1. Colourful Puppets: The vibrant colours and detailed designs of the puppets portray characters from folklore that add a touch to the performance.

2. Traditional Music: The live traditional music played on instruments creates a mesmerizing ambience that complements the puppetry.

3. Storytelling: Using puppets to convey stories is an art form that appeals to audiences of all ages whether through skits or captivating legends.

Here are some helpful tips for enriching experience:

1. Booking: Make sure to secure your tickets of time during busy tourist seasons to guarantee availability.
2. Arrival Time: Arrive at the theater early to settle into your seat and absorb the show atmosphere.
3. Photography: While flash photography is typically prohibited during the performance feel free to capture special moments before or after the show.
4. Language Assistance: Familiarize yourself with the show's themes or plotlines beforehand to enrich your understanding and enjoyment.
5. Ticket Information: For current ticket prices and seating options visit the theater's website or reach out directly.

Attending a water puppetry performance at the Golden Dragon Water Puppet Theater offers a journey into Vietnam's traditions and folklore. It appeals to history buffs as those seeking unique entertainment experiences. Don't miss out on this display during your visit to HCMC for an immersion in the mesmerizing world of Vietnamese water puppetry. The Water Puppetry Show was truly mesmerizing, showcasing skill and traditional tales through puppet dances, on water. The combination of music, vibrant puppets and skilled puppeteers created a truly captivating performance.

That evening we made our way, to a floating restaurant on the Sai Gon River for dinner. While savouring the dishes I found myself mesmerized by the twinkling city lights and the peaceful flow of the river. It was a conclusion to a day filled with exploration and immersion in culture.

As we made our way back, to Hotel Eden Garden, I took a moment to ponder the experiences of the day. Ho Chi Minh City had welcomed us with arms sharing its history and promising glimpses into its past, present and future. The day had been a journey filled with discoveries and culinary delights that would be cherished in our memories forever. Ho Chi Minh City you truly stole our hearts.

Saigon Princess - Luxury Dining Cruise, Dining at Saigon River Floating Restaurant

Location: 5 Nguyen Tat Thanh Street, District 4

When we boarded the Saigon River Floating Restaurant, in Ho Chi Minh City I was struck by the views that greeted me. The panoramic sight of the Saigon River with its glistening waters and verdant foliage along the banks set the scene for a dining adventure. Seated at a table strategically placed to capture the beauty I perused the menu brimming with Vietnamese dishes. From seafood delights to fragrant soups and tasty grilled meats the array of delights promised a sensory feast.

As we relished each mouthful of fare, I found myself not only indulging in the flavours but also soaking up the cultural ambience enveloping me. The soothing tunes of Vietnamese music wafted through the air enhancing the authenticity of my dining experience. At moments I was treated to enthralling performances such as water puppet shows that brought artistry vividly to life before my eyes. The romantic setting aboard the floating restaurant was undeniable. With lanterns casting a glow boat sways and a starlit sky above creating a magical atmosphere perfect for a special night out or a heartfelt celebration.

One standout moment, from my dining escapade was when I arranged a sunset cruise.

As the sun set below the horizon painting the sky with shades of orange and pink and casting a reflection, on the river waters we found ourselves completely mesmerized by the natural beauty that surrounded us. Throughout the night the welcoming team at the Saigon River Floating Restaurant made sure that every aspect of our dining experience was truly exceptional. Their friendly service, attention to detail and eagerness to cater to any requests added an extra layer of comfort and joy to our evening.

I would highly recommend booking your reservations in advance for dinner cruises or during tourist times to secure a spot in this one-of-a-kind floating restaurant. Whether you're a food lover, a couple, in search of romance or a traveller looking for an experience dining at the Saigon River Floating Restaurant guarantees a journey filled with local culture, delicious cuisine and breathtaking views along the iconic Saigon River.

"Travel makes one modest. You see what a tiny place you occupy in the world."

— Gustav Flaubert

~:Day 3:~ On the Way to Hoi An - Where Tranquillity meets Adventure.

We stayed at Dai An Phu Villa, Group 9, An Bang Beah, Cam An Ward, Hoi An

After enjoying a delightful breakfast and the warm hospitality of Eden Garden Hotel, we headed to the Tan Son Nhat International Airport for the next leg of our journey, bound for Hoi An. The hotel staff had graciously arranged for a cab to take us to the airport upon our request. However, upon arrival, we were met with an unexpected surprise – our flight, originally scheduled for 11:20 am as per Indochina time, had been delayed by a staggering six hours and twenty minutes and was now expected to depart at 6 pm. To add to the delay, the flight ended up taking off at 6:30 pm, leaving us with an entire day to fill at the airport.

Despite the disappointment of losing a day in Hoi An, we made the best of the situation and mingled with fellow passengers who were also affected by the delay. The airline crew handled the situation with professionalism and extended heartfelt apologies, even though the delay was beyond their control. We were eventually served dinner during the flight, and by around 8:50 pm, we finally arrived at our destination, Dai An Phu Villa.

Upon our arrival, we were warmly welcomed by the manager of the resort, Mr. Nguyễn Duy, who had been expecting us. The pre-booked cab from Da Nang Airport to the hotel provided us with a serene night journey, albeit one that caused us to miss out on a full day of exploring Hoi An City as originally planned.

Nestled in the serene charm of Hoi An, Dai An Phu Villa offered us a delightful retreat during our Vietnam adventure. This cosy bungalow, adorned with a lush garden, an inviting outdoor swimming pool, and a meticulously decorated terrace, provided the perfect setting for relaxation and exploration. Situated a mere 200 meters from the captivating An Bang Beach, the villa's tranquil ambience and proximity to nature were unparalleled. Our culinary journey was equally enchanting, with The Beach Restaurant offering a delectable array of Vietnamese delicacies and fresh seafood, complemented by a tempting selection of cocktails and snacks at the Bar. Our stay at Dai An Phu Villa was a harmonious blend of comfort, natural beauty, and culinary delights, making it a cherished memory of our time in Vietnam.

Despite the initial disappointment caused by a flight delay to Da Nang, which led to the cancellation of our planned activities, it turned out to be a beautiful and joyful moment that we will always cherish.

Instead of dwelling on the setback, we decided to embrace the evening and explore the local surroundings. With the allure of the beach beckoning, we embarked on a leisurely stroll along the shore after dinner, immersing ourselves in the enchanting night atmosphere of the sea and its surroundings.

There was a hint of apprehension as we ventured out into the unknown at 9:30 pm, but the spirit of adventure and curiosity prevailed. Initially hesitant, my wife and I found reassurance in the company of our Manager, Nguyễn Duy, who accompanied us on our walk. His words of assurance about the safety of Hoi An and Vietnam at night, coupled with the warm hospitality extended to tourists, eased our worries and filled us with excitement.

The night walk was a magical experience, filled with the soothing sounds of the waves and the gentle sea breeze. We felt welcomed by the locals we encountered along the way, adding to the charm of the evening. Despite being among the few tourists out that late, we felt a sense of belonging and exploration. Our dinner at The Beach Restaurant added to the memorable evening. We savoured plain rice, gravy noodles with meatballs and delectable local seafood, accompanied by refreshing drinks. While tempted by the offerings of hard drinks, I opted for a simple Coke out of respect for my wife's preferences, which added a touch of sweetness to the night. Overall, our impromptu adventure on the first day of our arrival in Hoi An was a beautiful and joyful moment that encapsulated the warmth, hospitality, and enchanting ambience of this charming Vietnamese town.

~:Day 4:~ Tour of the Golden Bridge and Ba Na Hills

On October 14, 2018, my wife and I embarked on a journey that would become one of the most cherished memories of our lives - our first foreign tour to Bana Hills in Danang, Vietnam. It was a trip we fondly refer to as our second honeymoon, filled with excitement, joy, and a sense of adventure.

Our first morning in Hoi An greeted us with a delightful breakfast spread showcasing the region's specialities: Hoi An's special buns, fluffy omelette, savoury chicken sausage, fresh fruits bursting with flavour, crisp green salad, accompanied by refreshing orange juice and a choice of tea or milk. It was a perfect start to our day, fuelling us with energy and excitement for the adventures ahead.

With some time to spare before our journey to Ba Na Hills, we indulged in a leisurely photo session around the resort, capturing the beauty of our surroundings. Our footsteps led us back to the sea beach, this time under the bright daylight, revealing a vibrant scene filled with people of all ages. What was a tranquil haven last night had transformed into a lively hub buzzing with excitement, joy, and laughter stretching across the beach as far as our eyes could see. Despite the lively atmosphere, our time was limited, prompting us to return to the resort sooner than we'd have liked. To our delight, our cab awaited us, ready to whisk us away to the much-anticipated highlight of our Hoi An journey – the Golden Bridge.

As the sun began its ascent over the vibrant city of Danang, Vietnam, my heart was filled with anticipation for the day ahead. It was a crisp morning when my spouse and I embarked on our much-awaited trip to Bana Hills, a place renowned for its breathtaking landscapes and captivating attractions. Little did we know that this journey would become a tapestry of unforgettable experiences, weaving together moments of tranquillity, awe, and sheer spectacle. The journey to Bana Hills started with a scenic drive from our hotel. We traversed through the bustling streets of Danang, catching glimpses of local life and the dynamic energy that permeated the city. The anticipation grew with every passing mile, knowing that we were heading towards a destination that promised to enchant and mesmerize.

Upon our arrival, at Bana Hills, we were instantly drawn in by the ambience and stunning views. The sun's warm rays bathed the scenery in a light. I initially chose to wear a light T-shirt and blue jeans, but a sudden change of heart led me to opt for a full red shirt and black jeans instead. Little did I realize that this outfit change would bring a touch of colour and character to our photos. As we reached the base of Bana we were greeted by the grandeur of landscapes and rolling hills. The thirty-minute cable car journey to the mountaintop was an exhilarating experience offering vistas of the surrounding nature. With each ascent, the urban hustle gradually faded away giving way to a panorama of beauty.

Our first stop brought us face-to-face with a row of bungalows designed in style. The intricate architectural details, artistic flair and exquisite decor left us awestruck—a testament to this place's past as part of Vietnam's colonial era under French rule. The joy we felt at Bana Hills is, beyond words. We spent an hour there capturing selfies and snapshots to cherish these moments forever. Every corner we ventured into every sight we marveled at felt like a scene, out of a dream.

In the snapshot we captured my joy and rejuvenated appearance were unmistakable. The presence of my wife beside me added a twinkle to the moment. Her inquisitive and delightful gaze towards our surroundings mirrored the spirit of adventure and discovery that united us.

Reflecting on that selfie today takes me back to that day at Bana Hills. The assurance and bravery I experienced stemmed not only from the scenery but also from the unwavering encouragement and affection of my wife. She motivated me to embrace experiences discover places and build enduring memories together. Our excursion to Bana Hills in

Danang, Vietnam will forever hold a spot in our hearts. It was a voyage filled with love, exploration and shared joy that deepened our connection and filled our souls with moments. Our initial visit was, to the French Village, a haven that transported us to another time period. The cobblestone pathways, charming European structures and lively hues evoked a vibe. We leisurely wandered through the village admiring the architecture of the buildings while immersing ourselves in the laid-back ambiance.

Ba Na Hills greeted us with a cool mountain climate, a stark contrast to the coastal breeze of Hoi An. The cable car ride to the hills was a thrilling experience, offering panoramic views of lush green landscapes. The Golden Bridge, held aloft by giant stone hands, was a sight to behold. We walked across this architectural marvel, feeling as though we were suspended in mid-air, surrounded by breathtaking scenery. The Golden Bridge, one of the highlights of our visit, was a marvel of contemporary architecture that seemed to defy gravity as it stretched across the lush hills. Walking on the bridge was an otherworldly experience, with stunning views of the surrounding mountains and the cool mountain breeze brushing against our skin. The Fantasy Park was another delightful discovery, offering a plethora of amusement rides, games, and activities. We embraced our inner child as we rode the carousel, played arcade games, and laughed together on thrilling rides. The park was alive with laughter and excitement, creating a joyful atmosphere that was infectious. As the day progressed, we explored the various attractions scattered throughout Bana Hills. The Linh Ung Pagoda, with its towering Buddha statue and serene surroundings, offered a moment of tranquillity and reflection.

Our journey culminated with a visit to the Bana Hills Gardens, a verdant oasis filled with colourful flowers, lush greenery, and panoramic views of the valley below. We found ourselves immersed in nature's embrace, breathing in the fresh mountain air and relishing the serenity of the surroundings. As the sun began its descent, casting a golden hue over Bana Hills, we reflected on the day's adventures. It was a journey filled with awe-inspiring moments, shared laughter, and a deep appreciation for the beauty of nature and human creativity. As we descended back to Danang, our hearts were full, and our minds were filled with memories that would last a lifetime. Bana Hills had woven its magic on us, leaving an indelible mark on our souls and igniting a desire to explore more of this wondrous world.

Following a day of exploration atop the hills we descended back, to Da Nang for a meal. The city's culinary offerings lived up to expectations as we delighted in delicacies that captured the flavours of Central Vietnam. Upon our evening arrival, in Hoi An we reminisced about the tranquil beach experiences, lively nightlife and exciting escapades that filled the two days. Hoi An truly won us over with its mix of relaxation and thrilling moments creating memories that will stay with us forever. We were eager to uncover gems and surprises awaiting us in this charming town.

A visit to the Marble Mountain Pagoda and Non-Nuoc Stone carving village

Da Nang City has many mountain temples where handmade architecture, natural sceneries and religious values are combined perfectly.

Exploring the wonders of Da Nang, my wife and I embarked on a memorable journey to the Marble Mountain Pagoda and Non-Nuoc Stone Carving Village. Our day had already been filled with excitement, starting with a captivating morning at Ba Na Hills and a satisfying lunch in Da Nang City. Now, we were ready to delve deeper into the cultural and artistic treasures this region has to offer.

Upon reaching the Marble Mountain Pagoda we were immediately captivated by the grandeur of the marble formations that defined the landscape. The pagoda itself nestled among the mountains emitted an aura of peace and spirituality. Ascending the hilltop allowed us to appreciate the carvings and ancient architectural details that adorned the pagoda—each element narrating tales of age traditions and beliefs.

From higher vantage points we were treated to sweeping views of Da Nang cityscape and its surrounding vistas—a spectacle that left us mesmerized by Vietnam's natural splendour. The tranquillity, within the pagoda, coupled with awe-inspiring panoramas made our visit an enriching experience.

After visiting the Non-Nuoc Stone Carving Village, known for its artisans' skill, in sculpting marble and stone we strolled around. Admired the incredible craftsmanship that goes into creating detailed statues, sculptures and decorative items from a raw stone. Interacting with the artisans allowed us to learn about their techniques and the cultural significance of their work. It was truly captivating to witness how these traditional methods have been handed down through generations preserving Vietnam's heritage of stone carving.

As the day came to an end we reflected on the beauty and cultural depth we encountered at both the Marble Mountain Pagoda and Non Nuoc Stone Carving Village. It was a day filled with exploration, inspiration and a deep appreciation for the artistry and history that define this captivating region of Da Nang.

Following our adventures exploring Da Nangs attractions, we happily returned to Dai An Phu Villa in Hoi An. Our cab dropped us off gracefully at the resort's inviting entrance where familiar faces welcomed us back, to the tranquil ambience we cherished. In the evening our thoughtful manager had a surprise waiting for us.

He planned an evening stroll, in the Old Town of Hoi An a UNESCO World Heritage site known for its timeless allure and historical importance.

As night fell over Hoi An the town turned into a captivating paradise. We explored the heart of the Old Town, where lanterns lit up the streets and the scent of street food wafted through the air. The night market enticed us with a variety of souvenirs and local crafts. For dinner, we enjoyed a meal at a riverside eatery savoring specialties like Cao Lau and White Rose Dumplings. The atmosphere was enchanting with traditional music providing a backdrop to our meal. Following dinner, we took a boat ride along the Thu Bon River winding through the town. The glimmering lanterns mirrored in the water creating a romantic ambiance. It was an evening to remember blending culture, cuisine and companionship

Our final day in Hoi An started with a peaceful morning walk along the shores of Hoi An Beach at 6 am. The calming sound of waves crashing against the shore and the gentle sea breeze served as an awakening, for my senses.

As I strolled on the sand feeling refreshed by the beach ambience I gathered seashells as keepsakes and savoured the tranquillity.

My wife however seemed weary from our jam-packed schedule the day. We had rushed through a tour of Da Nang City, Ba Na Hills and Hoi An City in a day, due to delays. Recognizing her need for rest I decided to explore the seaside on my own a brief walk from Dai An Phu Villa.

The morning at the beach was truly magical. The sun rose gently in the east casting a glow over the glistening waters. With others, I took pleasure in a leisurely stroll along the shore and occasionally dipped my toes into the refreshing seawater. During my walk, I struck up a chat with a gentleman from England who admired the pattern of my yellow and black cotton shirt. Inspired by Shantiniketans Batik style. We shared stories. Travel tales about his time, in Kolkata and Shantiniketan.

As the morning went on I said goodbye to my friend. Took a short walk, around the local market. I bought some Dragon fruits and litchis to enjoy later. When I got back to the villa my wife was already up for breakfast. We enjoyed our meal together while talking about the morning we had by the beach. As we returned to our villa I was welcomed by the smell of a traditional Vietnamese breakfast. A hot bowl of pho along with fruits and fragrant coffee was a way to start an exciting day of exploration.

After breakfast and some downtime, we got ready for our adventure. Luckily our flight from Da Nang to Hanoi was, on time promising a travel experience ahead.

♣ ♣ ♣

"The real voyage of discovery consists not in seeking new landscapes, but in having new eyes."

— **Marcel Proust**

~:Day 5:~ Hanoi Unveiled : A Day of Heritage and Flavour

We stayed at Hanoi Nostalgia Hotel & Spa, 13 Phố Lương Ngọc Quyến Hàng Buồm 11010 Hà Nội

Arriving in Hanoi welcomed us with a warm afternoon and a lively cityscape full of excitement and curiosity. The cab ride, to Hotel Nostalgia, was pleasant allowing us to catch glimpses of the city's sights, including the Nhật Tân Bridge over the Red River with its modern cable-stayed structure showcasing Hanoi's progress.

Upon arrival at the hotel, we took a moment to relax after our journey from Da Nang. The excitement of exploring Hanoi was tangible, especially knowing that our guide, Ms. Water was ready to take us on a city tour.

Our first visit was to the house on 87 Ma May Street offering insights, into Hanoi's history and architectural legacy. The detailed wooden carvings, traditional design and vintage furnishings provided a peek into the lives of residents. Each room seemed to echo tales of yesteryears showcasing the skill and care put into creating such a residence.

We then strolled through the French Quarter admiring the splendor of Cathedral Church and the serene beauty of Hoan Kiem Lake that captured our hearts. The beautiful combination of architecture and Vietnamese traditions was truly captivating, with each building and monument narrating the rich history of Hanoi. We enjoyed a walk around the lake immersing ourselves in the atmosphere of daily life in Hanoi. A visit to the Hoa Lo Prison offered a solemn enlightening glimpse into Vietnam's past showcasing the resilience and spirit of its people.

As we meandered along the Hoan Kiem Lake, an encounter with schoolchildren added a heartwarming touch to our day in Hanoi. Our guide, Ms. Water introduced us to these youngsters who had gathered at the park for some moments. I was pleasantly surprised by their command of English and their eagerness to engage in conversation. When I mentioned India their faces lit up with joy as they shared their admiration for Bollywood stars like Shahrukh Khan and Amir Khan as their love for the popular TV show CID. During our chat, their dreams and goals unfolded before us. From aspiring explorers to astronauts or computer engineers, their enthusiasm and curiosity were truly inspiring.

Amidst our evening walk, we stumbled upon a street vendor selling mangoes seasoned with spices and sauce. The sight and smell instantly brought back memories of my childhood thinking about enjoying mango pickles despite my mother's disapproval. It was a moment that reminded me of family gatherings and delicious meals shared with loved ones. With a grin I remembered the saying, 'Let children learn to eat everything' a sentiment passed down by my grandparents who encouraged our explorations.

I couldn't resist the urge to ask Ms. Water to get some of those treats for us. We enjoyed the spicy mangoes as we strolled leisurely around the lake savoring not only the flavors but also the simple pleasures of unexpected encounters and treasured memories.

After a long walk, our hunger led us to Pho Bien, a known seafood restaurant where we feasted on an array of dishes relishing the ocean's freshness in every bite. To end our day on a note we delighted in the egg coffee at Ca Phe Pho Co, a hidden gem located in Hanoi's heart. The creamy consistency and rich aroma of the coffee provided the conclusion, to our days escapades.

As the evening, in Hanoi came to an end we said goodbye to our guide, Ms. Water at the hotel entrance. Her knowledge, stories and company added depth to our exploration of the city streets giving us an understanding of Hanois culture and history. To show our appreciation for her time and the enriching experiences she shared with us I offered her a token of gratitude in the form of money. However, I was surprised when Ms. Water politely declined, explaining that their guiding service is focused on learning and education making it against their principles to accept gifts.

I was truly impressed by her dedication to education. Her commitment to offering experiences to visitors like us. Her humility and enthusiasm for sharing knowledge struck a chord with me emphasizing the importance of exchange and respect in travel encounters. As we went our ways I found myself reflecting on the connections we had established during our stay in Hanoi thanks in large part to the kindness and generosity shown by individuals such, as Ms. Water. Her refusal of payment spoke volumes about the spirit of hospitality and sincere care that defined our journey through Vietnam.

Upon returning to our hotel reminiscing about the buildings, streets and delicious food we encountered in Hanoi we felt excited knowing that our exploration of the city had just started. From exploring houses to wandering through streets and savouring local cuisine each experience deeply touched us and hinted at the many more exciting moments awaiting us in the upcoming days.

~:Day 6:~ Tour of Ha Long Bay

We stayed at La Paz Resort/ Tuan Chau Resort Ha Long, Đường Ngọc Châu, Tuan Chau Island

Our trip, to Halong Bay, was a mix of surprises and exceptional hospitality that truly made our journey unforgettable. It all started with a twist of fate when unexpectedly our booked deluxe room in the resort building by the seafront was unavailable. However, what seemed like a disappointment turned out to be a break as we were warmly welcomed into a lovely two-story bungalow nestled among the hills offering stunning views and peaceful serenity.

The staff's warm welcome and the special treatment we received during the music concert and evening meal added a touch of luxury to our experience making us feel incredibly special. Despite some worries about being far from the area in our new accommodation, we found ourselves enchanted by the tranquil surroundings and beautiful views. Our spacious room on the floor facing east gave us vistas of the town and beach below creating a charming backdrop for our stay.

Upon reaching La Paz Resort on Taun Sua Island around noon we excitedly left most of our luggage after storing some at Nostalgia Hotel & Spa, in Hanoi.

As we joined the group for our cruise, in Halong Bay excitement filled us as we set off to explore this UNESCO World Heritage site and one of the seven wonders of the world.

Cruising through the emerald waters on our boat we were captivated by the towering limestone islands adorned with rainforests each shrouded in an aura that whispered ancient tales. The hidden caves and grottoes unveiled a world of marvels tempting us to delve into the captivating beauty of Halong Bay. Our time in Halong Bay was a blend of discoveries breathtaking natural beauty and warm hospitality leaving us with treasured memories and a newfound admiration for the diverse landscapes of our planet.

Stepping onto the Deluxe cruise from Tuan Chua Island harbour we were welcomed with drinks that set the stage for an unforgettable journey, through Halong Bay. Following a reception we were escorted to the restaurant on the front deck offering panoramic views of the sea through its expansive windows. The gentle breeze added to the atmosphere as we prepared for a treat.

The dining experience was truly exceptional featuring an eight-course lunch showcasing a fusion of flavours.

The day menu featured a combination of cucumber and tomato salad succulent prawns, Halong famous stir-fried squid, with celery crispy Vietnamese spring rolls, flavorful stir-fried chicken with mushrooms fish in a delightful tomato sauce, a mix of stir-fried veggies fragrant steamed rice and a sweet finale of fresh seasonal fruits.

After enjoying this meal we headed up to the rooftop of the two-story cruise ship. There we found a long lawn shaded by greenery and cosy chairs waiting for us. It was the spot to take in the beauty of Halong Bay. The cool sea breeze mingling with subtle fog and bright sunshine added to the ambiance.

As we cruised through the bay surrounded by floating rocks and verdant islands the picturesque view was like something out of a photographer's fantasy. The rooftop provided a backdrop, for capturing moments and scenic selfies against the stunning natural backdrop of Halong Bay wonders. Standing on the edge of Halong Bay filled me with excitement for a day of exploration and adventure. The prospect of cruising through this bay for 4 to 4.5 hours with plenty of activities left me eagerly looking forward to it.

It was an experience combining food with the breathtaking natural beauty of Halong Bay, in Vietnam.

As our boat started its journey we mesmerized by the scenery all around us. The limestone islands and islets rose from the waters like protectors each with its own unique form and tale. Every corner we turned in the bay revealed a sight of natural splendour. One of the parts of our trip was the guided tour that showcased many famous landmarks. We were in awe of the towering stone formations shaped by years of wind and water erosion while also learning about the folklore and stories that define Halong Bays' past. Our visit to Heavenly Palace Cave left me feeling amazed as we stepped into its chambers adorned with stalactites and stalagmites. The interplay of light and darkness, within created an atmosphere underscoring why this cave is celebrated as a marvel of nature.

The excitement continued with a kayaking adventure to explore the Ba Hang area and nearby fishing communities. Cruising peacefully in our kayaks, on the tranquil waters we were surrounded by a sense of calm and peace. The towering limestone karsts above us inspired awe and admiration for the beauty of nature. Some of our travellers opted for a bamboo boat ride gently gliding through the waters to explore the charming fishing villages scattered along the bay. It offered a peek into the lives of fishermen with their vibrant boats swaying gently on the calm waves against the backdrop of Halong Bays' timeless charm.

As we headed back to shore as the day waned I found myself pondering over the allure of Halong Bay. Its natural magnificence, intertwined with encounters had left an enduring impression, on my spirit. Halong Bay had indeed lived up to its reputation as a place brimming with magic and marvel a treasure trove waiting to be discovered at every turn.

Approaching the conclusion of our cruise through Halong Bay we were treated to a delightful afternoon tea service. It was a moment of savouring tea while soaking in the glimpses of the breathtaking landscapes surrounding us. As we unwound two amiable ladies approached us displaying artefacts crafted from sea shells, pearls and oysters.

My wife fell in love with a pearl necklace, as a keepsake of our time in this charming place. Meanwhile, I chose to get some keychains featuring pictures of Ha Long Bay and other famous tourist spots in Vietnam. Even though we had already gathered quite a few souvenirs from our visits to Ho Chi Minh City, Da Nang and Hoi An we couldn't resist picking up a few items to cherish the memories.

When we arrived back at the port around 5 pm our transition to the leg of our journey went smoothly. A car was waiting to take us to our resort, where our room was ready and welcoming. After unpacking and freshening up we headed over to the building at around 6:30 pm for an evening ahead.

The night came alive with a captivating music performance that filled the air with melodies echoing the beauty of Halong Bay. The atmosphere was enchanting with twinkling lights adding a hint of romance, to the night. After the concert, we enjoyed a dinner featuring Vietnamese dishes that delighted our taste buds and enriched our travel experiences.

The day, in Halong Bay ended beautifully filled with adventure, new discoveries and a deep dive into the culture. As we settled into our room for the night a sense of gratitude washed over me for the memories we made and the precious souvenirs we collected during our journey.

"Once a year, go someplace you've never been before."

— Dalai Lama

~:Day 7:~ Returns back to Hanoi

After enjoying a stay, at La Paz Resort on Taun Sua Island in Halong Bay my spouse and I set off on our journey back to Hanoi. The morning following our 7:30 am breakfast we decided to take in the beauty of Taun Sua Island one time by going for a walk. The sun was shining brightly casting a glow over the surroundings as we leisurely walked towards the harbor. Upon reaching the harbour memories of our trip to Halong Bay came rushing back. We reminisced about the awe-inspiring cruise through the captivating islands brimming with excitement and adventure at every corner. Our time in Vietnam was coming to an end. The memories we created together will forever be cherished in our hearts. After spending an hour soaking up the islands charm we made our way back to La Paz Resort. With our bags packed from the night we quickly checked out. Awaited the e-rickshaw arranged by the resort to transport us to the main building for departure procedures.

The team at Hanoi Transfer Service (HTS) played a role in organizing our Ha Long Bay tour, which we had arranged online from India along, with all of our accommodations at destinations.

We were pleasantly surprised to discover that HTS had arranged for a four seater car, for both parts of our journey from Hanoi to Ha Long Bay. Travelling in comfort and style added a layer of enjoyment to our already memorable trip.

When we arrived at the building our car was waiting for us ready to take us to Hanoi. Saying goodbye to the beauty of Ha Long Bay was a mix of emotions. We were thankful for the wonderful memories we had made during our time there. On the way to Hanoi, we reminisced about the adventures and happiness of our Halong Bay Cruise journey that would always hold a place in our travel memories.

Around 3 pm we reached Hotel Nostalgia Hanoi. Took a break for lunch at a spot along the journey. After arriving at the hotel we collected our luggage from the cloakroom. Headed to our room. Later in the evening, we went out for a walk. Feeling slightly hungry we decided to stop by a café, for some snacks and coffee. As dusk approached the streets lit up with captivating lights and the city buzzed with evening activity.

The local market was bustling with activity as traders geared up for the evening drawing in both residents and travellers from, around the world. The atmosphere was magical as we strolled through the streets soaking in the sights and sounds of Hanoi as night fell. It served as an introduction to the nightlife and busy markets that give Hanoi its charm.

The hotel staff recommended we visit the Hanoi Night Market emphasizing it as a must-see attraction. Luckily the market was a walk away. Since it was our last night in Hanoi and Vietnam we were determined to make the most of it by exploring on foot.

During our stay at Hotel Nostalgia Hanoi, I didn't notice the functional bathroom slippers they provided. What stood out to me was their design – they didn't retain water when wet due to perforations that allowed moisture to escape easily. Not only were they practical, but they were also incredibly comfortable without causing any discomfort or irritation to my feet. Impressed, by their practicality I decided to buy a pair to bring back home as a memento.

When I asked about these slippers at the hotel's desk I was told they could be found at the night market and, at a good price too. With this goal in mind, our first mission at the market was to locate these slippers. After a search we stumbled upon a store that had the kind of slippers I wanted. Without any delay I bought them.

The Hanoi Night Market, which operates every Friday, Saturday and Sunday night from 8 p.m. to 11 p.m. spans about 3 kilometers from Dong Kinh Nghia Thuc Square to the entrance of Dong Xuan Market. What immediately caught my attention was how accessible and welcoming it felt – entry was free. The streets were blocked off from traffic creating a pedestrian environment where visitors and locals mingled freely. The market was brimming with treasures featuring stalls offering a range of goods. From crafted handicrafts showcasing Vietnam's cultural heritage to elegant ceramics, trendy clothing and unique mementoes there was something to catch everyone's eye. The prices were fair making it an ideal spot, for both bargain hunters and souvenir enthusiasts.

As we delved into the renowned Weekend Night Market it filled us with anticipation.

We soon found ourselves fully immersed in the atmosphere of this known night market. As the sun set below the horizon the busy streets came to life with a mix of colours, sounds and smells promising an evening of exploration and enjoyment. The market transformed into a hub of stalls, local vendors, tourists and residents offering a night filled with cultural experiences, arts and crafts and delicious food. It was, like discovering a treasure trove of delights with stalls showcasing a range of goods. Our attention was immediately caught by the array of products on display. From crafted handicrafts to ceramics and trendy clothing items there were plenty of choices available. The souvenirs priced between 100,000 to 200,000 VND stood out as gifts for our loved ones' homes. The quality of the handicrafts was truly impressive making it a go to place for souvenir shopping. Apart from shopping opportunities the market was also a paradise for food lovers. The enticing aroma of specialities, like Bun Thang, La

Vong grilled fish, Pho noodle soup, Banh mi sandwiches and Bun cha meatballs filled the air.

I couldn't resist treating myself to these dishes with prices starting at a VND 15000 creating a delightful culinary journey.

We explored a variety of dishes from steaming bowls of Pho to flavorful Banh mi sandwiches and sizzling skewers of grilled meat.

The evenings, on Saturdays and Sundays at the market were full of life with live performances enhancing the atmosphere. Vietnamese opera, traditional and modern music shows and occasional appearances by artists entertained both locals and tourists. The vibrant energy and heartfelt performances left a lasting impression.

Amidst the city life of Hanoi, one thing that stood out was how families made time for weekend fun. Despite the crowds, there was a sense of unity and happiness, in the air.

We came across a group of artists preparing for a street performance as children eagerly awaited the show with their parents. It was heartening to see them sitting on the pavement fully engrossed in the entertainment while their parents watched over them. Nearby musicians tuned their instruments adding to the excitement and celebratory vibe. We paused our exploration to take in this scene immersing ourselves in the street performance and capturing moments with our cameras. The energy was contagious. For those moments we were transported into the world of the play. Laughing and enjoying alongside others in attendance.

In a corner, a cluster of musicians performed captivating melodies on their flutes filling the surroundings with music. The enchanting tunes seemed to transport us into a world of harmony, where we were momentarily lost in the spell of the music. These spontaneous encounters, with art and culture enriched our visit, to the Hanoi Night Market showcasing the community spirit that thrives amidst the city's lively streets.

Surrounded by the energy of the Hanoi Night Market we immersed ourselves in the scene of street vendors and shopkeepers vying for attention. While strolling through the lanes with my spouse I couldn't resist sharing with her the flavors of street food. Despite her hesitation she eventually. We decided to treat ourselves to an array of Vietnamese delicacies. We savoured a bowl of Pho and indulged in a Banh mi sandwich. Relished some grilled meat as we eagerly embraced the cuisine. The Pho soup—a dish—was a delightful fusion of bone broth, rice noodles and thinly sliced beef.

The dish was served with bean sprouts, fresh herbs, lime wedges and chilli peppers enhancing its flavours and freshness. We discovered that Pho can be made with chicken or vegetables to cater to tastes. Trying the Banh mi sandwich was a surprise. The crispy crust and soft interior of the baguette were generously filled with ingredients. We chose the Banh mi thit with meat fillings, pickled vegetables and cilantro. The vegetarian option featured tofu and fresh veggies, for a mix of textures and flavours. As someone who enjoys grilled meats like tandooris, I couldn't resist tasting the Vietnamese grilled meat that reminded me of our tandoori dishes. The charred flavours blended perfectly with the spices for a mouthwatering combination. To cool down after all the excitement we enjoyed treats on sticks from a street vendor to our Indian kulfi malai – a refreshing conclusion to our culinary exploration.

Our experience sampling street food was a fusion of flavours, textures and scents that gave us a deeper admiration, for Hanoi's culinary traditions.

Our time, in Vietnam concluded perfectly with a mix of food and cultural exploration. While we savored Vietnamese street eats the lively Hanoi Night Market only heightened our hunger prompting us to seek out a restaurant for dinner. Following a search we found Tandoor Restaurant close to our hotel. Yearning for tastes my wife and I ordered rice freshly baked naan bread, creamy chicken korma and refreshing mango lassi. The meal at Tandoor Restaurant was a reminder of home flavours we missed while travelling evoking memories of our country. Especially since our last Indian feast was in Ho Chi Minh City days before.

To enhance the experience further we were pleasantly surprised to learn that the owner of Tandoor Restaurant hailed from Digha, our hometown in

Bengal. Meeting someone, with the roots and language felt like reconnecting with family in a place.

We had a chat, with him talking about his business ventures and my profession while reminiscing about our tour adventures. He also shared some family stories adding a touch to our dinner. Around 10 pm the hotel manager reminded us to be by 10:30 so we said goodbye to the owner. Quickly made our way back to the hotel appreciating the warm connection and delicious meal that brought a sense of home to our journey in Vietnam.

To sum up our time at Hanoi Weekend Night Market was a dive, into the city's culture, craftsmanship, food scene and lively entertainment offerings. It's definitely a must-see for anyone wanting to soak in the energy of Hanoi's nightlife and shopping experience.

~:Day 8:~ Return journey to Kolkata

Certainly, the unwavering support of my wife instilled in me the confidence and bravery to embark on this journey, to Vietnam, a memory that I will always hold dear. As we bid adieu to the captivating land of Vietnam our hearts brimmed with memories and a newfound admiration for its charm. Our time there was truly transformative underscoring the rooted connection between India and Vietnam and the resilience of the spirit in times of hardship.

The last day in Vietnam was filled with moments and experiences that will forever be etched in our hearts. The previous night had been a whirlwind of delight as we wandered through the night market immersing ourselves in a blend of global cultures savoring Vietnamese traditions and delicacies and reveling in the harmonious mix of local music and international vibes. Whether watching street performances showcasing Vietnam's heritage or relishing Indian dishes at Tandoor each instant felt like a precious gem.

Our morning commenced with a breakfast at 7:50 am in the dining hall. The room hummed with travellers, from corners of the globe creating a tapestry of diverse cultures and languages. The air carried hints of blooms accompanied by Vietnamese melodies playing softly in the background.

The breakfast selection was an assortment of rice, noodles, salads, bread, fruits, eggs, meats and fish that catered to all tastes. Skilled chefs prepared made-to-order omelettes with a touch that added to the dining experience. Our meal was complemented by a variety of beverages such, as fruit juice, milk, tea and coffee setting the tone for a productive day ahead.

Following our satisfying breakfast we ventured into the hotel's terrace garden to capture memories through photographs. Although I had planned on taking a swim in the pool feelings of embarrassment and my wife's hesitation deterred us due to our lack of swimming expertise.

Upon checking out from the hotel at 9 am with farewells to the welcoming staff we made our way to Noiboi International Airport for our 12:10 pm flight to Singapore. Boarding our Singapore Airlines flight ensured a journey with appointed seating and a delectable lunch served onboard.

As we soared above Singapore harbour in awe-inspiring fashion the view of waters teeming with life, below us painted a picture. Capturing these mesmerizing sights through photography allowed us to appreciate nature's wonders from above.

Upon our arrival, at Singapore International Airport at 3:02 pm we excitedly boarded our flight bound for

Kolkata at 7 pm anticipating a taste of home with a dinner served during the journey. Despite battling jet lag and the weariness from a flight our travel experience was enriched by captivating sights and delectable culinary offerings.

As we landed at Netaji Subhash Chandra Bose International Airport in Kolkata, around 11:10 pm (IST) we reflected on our trip with a sense of satisfaction appreciative of the meaningful experiences and cherished memories we had gathered along the expedition.

"If you're twenty-two, physically fit, hungry to learn and be better, I urge you to travel – as far and widely as possible."

— Anthony Bourdain

Epilogue

Our journey, to Vietnam was truly remarkable and eye-opening. We were captivated by the country's resilience in embracing its culture while moving towards a future. The kindness and friendliness of the locals added a touch to our trip. As we left Vietnam we carried with us cherished memories and a newfound appreciation for the beauty of diversity. Vietnam has left a mark on our hearts. We eagerly look forward to returning to this enchanting land.

Exploring known parts of Vietnam over eight days was an enriching adventure that allowed me to delve into the country's history, traditions and natural splendour. The warmth of the people and the stunning landscapes have left a lasting impression on my heart. Upon returning to Kolkata I not only brought back memories but a deep connection to this incredible nation. This experience emphasized how travel can broaden our perspectives and enrich our lives inspiring me to seek treasures in destinations, in the future—places filled with untold stories and unforgettable moments.

Reflecting on our journey through Vietnam I am filled with awe at the magic of discovering places and uncovering gems. Each day was a blend of tradition modern aspirations and the resilient spirit of a nation that has courageously faced challenges head-on.

When I think of the streets of Hanoi, the beauty of Ha Long Bay and the rich history of Hoi An it's truly amazing to see how diverse and captivating our world can be.

Exploring off the paths allowed us to uncover gems, in Vietnam, where we encountered moments that etched unforgettable memories in our journey – sharing meals with locals stumbling upon talented artisans unexpectedly or simply immersing ourselves in nature's tranquillity. These experiences strengthened my bond with this country and its people in ways I never thought possible.

Traveling goes beyond ticking destinations off a checklist; it's about forming lasting connections gaining perspectives and embracing the tapestry that makes our world so colorful. Vietnam has left a mark on my heart evoking not memories but a fresh sense of wonder for what lies beyond familiar horizons. As I conclude this chapter in my travel diary I am grateful for the shared memories, the wisdom. The relationships forged along our journey. Even though our exploration of Vietnam has come to an end the memories of its allure, resilience and warmth will linger on within me as inspiration, for travels and a reminder of the enchantment found in discovering places. Until we meet again in Vietnam, xin chào và tạm biệt, hello and goodbye.

I would like to conclude my travelogue with a poem in the form of a Cinquain.

Vietnam

Travel
Exotic, Quaint,
Planning, Knowing, Relaxing,
Picturesque journey I ever had,
Foreign.

Hoi An,
Ancient, Town,
Enjoying, Exploring, Shooting,
Carrying history in itself,
Seashore.

Da Nang,
Romantic, Scenic,
Travelling, Enjoying, Alluring,
Mesmerized by the Golden Bridge,
Midpoint.

Cuisine,
Mouth watery, Delish,

Eating, enjoying, watching,
Bot Chien, Banh Khot, Goi Cuon are few,
Menu.

A few pieces of information related to Vietnam gathered from the Internet before planning my trip to Vietnam.

Discovering Vietnam's vibrant seasons: No matter when you choose to visit Vietnam, this enchanting country promises unforgettable experiences, each season offering its own unique charm. Throughout the year, Vietnam offers a tapestry of experiences, each month unveiling a new facet of this captivating country.

<u>The peak season</u>

When planning your journey through Vietnam, consider the vibrant high season of July and August. These months beckon travellers with bustling cities, pristine coastlines, and a rich cultural tapestry. However, be prepared for a surge in prices, especially along the picturesque coastlines. To secure the best accommodations, it's wise to book well in advance. During this period, the entire nation, with the exception of the far north, basks in warm and humid conditions, occasionally interrupted by dramatic summer monsoon showers.

July – High season and Spectacular Pyrotechnics.

July kicks off the high season, with rising accommodation prices and increased crowds, especially in coastal areas. The Danang International Fireworks Festival in late June and early July adds extra excitement with breathtaking pyrotechnic displays.

August – Peak Tourism and Cultural Celebration

August is the peak month for tourism, drawing both domestic and international visitors. Flights and accommodations should be booked well in advance. Hot weather prevails, and cultural festivals like Trung Nguyen and the Children's Festival offer colourful and festive experiences.

Embracing the shoulder season

For those seeking a more tranquil Vietnam experience, the shoulder season spanning from December to March is a delightful choice. During this time, you'll encounter drier weather compared to the humid summer months. However, do pack accordingly, especially if you plan to explore the northern regions, where chilly temperatures prevail. In the far south, expect clear skies and abundant sunshine. This season offers a pleasant visit to iconic cities like Hanoi and Ho Chi Minh City, with reliable weather and comfortable temperatures. Worth noting is the Tet festival, typically falling in late January or early February, when the entire country comes alive, albeit with a rise in hotel prices.

December –Preparing for Holidays

December starts quietly but grows busier toward mid-month, especially in popular tourist destinations. Book accommodations well in advance for the Christmas break. The south experiences steamy weather, while the north can get chilly. Although not a national holiday, Christmas Day is celebrated throughout Vietnam, offering a unique experience in places like Phát Diệm and HCMC, where midnight Mass draws thousands.

January – Welcoming Winter Wonders

As the calendar flips to January, Vietnam experiences a diverse range of climates. While the far north shivers with the possibility of snow, the southern regions offer milder temperatures. This month, immerse yourself in the delightful Dalat Flower Festival, a spectacular event featuring lavish floral displays, music, fashion shows, and a lively wine festival.

February – Tết and Regional Contrasts

February brings a stark contrast between the northern and southern regions. The north, north of Danang, encounters chilly "Chinese winds" with overcast skies, while the south enjoys sunny and warm days. However, travel during Tết, the Vietnamese New Year, can be challenging due to high demand for transportation and business closures. Keep in mind that Tết may sometimes fall in late January.

March – The Rise of Temperatures

Grey skies and cool temperatures continue to affect areas north of Hội An in March, but as the month progresses, the thermometer begins to rise. Meanwhile, in the south, the dry season starts to draw to a close. Coffee enthusiasts should head to Buôn Ma Thuột for the annual coffee festival, where growers, grinders, blenders, and coffee aficionados gather for a vibrant celebration.

Exploring the low season

Vietnam's low season, spanning April to June and September to November, invites adventurous travellers to embrace a more unpredictable climate. During this transitional period between winter and summer, or summer and winter, you'll encounter a mix of splendid sunny days and occasional rainfall. This is an ideal time for those who prefer to avoid the tourist crowds or plan to embark on a comprehensive tour of the country. Remarkably, the weather remains relatively agreeable throughout Vietnam during these months, making it an excellent opportunity to uncover the nation's hidden gems.

April – Festivals and Favourable Weather

April is an ideal time to explore Vietnam, as the winter rainy season typically recede. This month offers a plethora of festivals, including the Hue Festival, featuring art, theatre, music, circus performances, and the solemn Thanh Minh (Holiday of the Dead), where ancestral traditions are honoured throughout the country.

May – Tranquil Skies and Buddha's Blessing

May is perfect for touring central and northern Vietnam, with clear skies and warm days. Sea temperatures become inviting, and tourism remains relatively quiet. Embrace the vibrant Phóng Sinh festival, celebrating Buddha's Birth, Enlightenment, and Death with lively street processions and lanterns adorning pagodas.

June – Beat the Crowds and Coastal Retreats

June is a fantastic time to explore Vietnam, just before the peak domestic tourism season. While humidity can be challenging, coastal retreats offer respite. The Nha Trang Sea Festival, held biannually in early June, fills the city with street festivals, photography exhibitions, sports events, and cultural displays.

September – The Start of the Low Season

September marks the beginning of Vietnam's second annual low season. Coastal resorts are less crowded, and the weather becomes milder. Vietnam National Day celebrations on September 2 and Hanoi Pride festivities add to the vibrant atmosphere.

October – Ideal for Northern Hikes

October is an excellent time to visit the far north, with clear skies and mild temperatures conducive to hiking. The central region experiences the onset of winter winds and rain, while the south remains dry. Enjoy moon cakes during Trung Thu (Mid-Autumn Festival), a delightful tradition celebrated across the country.

November – Sunny Skies and Cultural Celebrations

November is a splendid time to explore HCMC, Mũi Né, the Mekong Delta, and islands like Phú Quốc, where sunny skies dominate. The Khmer Ok Om

Bok Festival in the Mekong Delta features colourful boat races, showcasing the local culture.

Here are some do's and don'ts to keep in mind while travelling to Vietnam as a tourist:

Do's

1. **Respect local customs:** Be aware of and respect Vietnamese customs and traditions, such as removing shoes before entering someone's home or temple, dressing modestly when visiting religious sites, and using both hands when giving or receiving items.

2. **Learn basic Vietnamese phrases:** Learning a few basic Vietnamese phrases such as greetings, "thank you," and "please" can go a long way in showing respect and building rapport with locals.

3. **Be open to try local cuisine:** Vietnamese cuisine is diverse and delicious. Don't hesitate to try local dishes like pho, banh mi, and fresh spring rolls from street vendors or local restaurants.

4. **Negotiate politely:** When shopping at markets or dealing with vendors, it's common to negotiate prices. However, do so politely and with a friendly attitude.

5. **Dress appropriately:** While Vietnam is relatively liberal in terms of dress, especially in urban areas, it's still respectful to dress modestly, especially when visiting religious sites like temples and

pagodas.

6. **Carry some cash amount:** While credit cards are widely accepted in cities and tourist areas, having some cash on hand is useful, especially in rural areas or smaller establishments.

7. **Be mindful of scams:** Like any tourist destination, be cautious of scams such as overcharging, fake products, or unofficial tour operators. Research reputable businesses and be wary of too-good-to-be-true deals.

8. **Respect the environment:** Vietnamese people love their country very much. They also maintain cleanliness across the country. Also, Vietnam has beautiful natural landscapes, sea beaches and streams. Respect the environment by not littering, following designated trails, and supporting eco-friendly activities.

Don'ts

1. **Don't disrespect cultural symbols:** Avoid disrespecting national symbols, religious artefacts, or customs. For example, never step on money (which features national leaders) or point your feet at people or religious objects.

2. **Don't engage in public displays of affection:** Public displays of affection are generally frowned

upon in Vietnamese culture, especially in rural areas or conservative communities.

3. **Don't discuss sensitive topics:** Avoid discussing sensitive topics such as politics, religion, or the Vietnam War unless you are well-informed and the conversation is welcomed by locals.

4. **Don't haggle too aggressively:** While negotiating prices is common, being overly aggressive or confrontational during haggling can be seen as rude. Especially in local markets, you will find prices vary from stall to stall. Don't engage in any arguments rather politely say you cannot afford it or you would like to buy a little cheaper.

5. **Don't take photos without permission:** Vietnamese people are generous and they happily allow others to shoot videos with them or take snaps with them. But, always ask for permission before taking photos of people, especially in rural areas or when photographing religious ceremonies.

6. **Don't ignore health precautions:** Like every country, Vietnam has also some common health risk factors like malaria etc. Carry necessary medicines and vaccinations. Be cautious with

street food, drink bottled water, and avoid unnecessary physical activities if your health is not permitted to do that.

7. **Don't be offended by directness:** The Vietnamese communication style can be direct and speedy, which might come across as rude to some people. Try to understand cultural differences and don't take offense too easily.

8. **Don't use offensive gestures:** Avoid using offensive gestures or body language, as these can be misinterpreted and cause offence.

Some useful tips for travelling to Vietnam

Visa Requirements: Check the visa requirements well in advance. Vietnam typically requires a visa for most visitors, although some nationalities may be exempt for short stays. Vietnam offers an on-arrival visa for selected countries and for others, it is needed to be pre-booked.

Weather Considerations: Vietnam has a diverse climate. Check the weather conditions for the specific regions you plan to visit, as the weather can vary significantly from north to south.

Health Precautions: Ensure you have the necessary vaccinations before travelling. Consider health insurance that covers medical evacuation, especially if you plan to engage in adventurous activities.

Currency: The official currency is the Vietnamese Dong (VND). While major tourist areas may accept USD or EUR, it's best to have local currency for smaller purchases and in more rural areas.

Local Customs: Familiarize yourself with local customs and etiquette. For example, it's polite to remove your shoes before entering someone's home or a temple.

Transportation: Vietnam has various transportation options including taxis, motorbikes, and public buses. Use reputable taxi companies and negotiate fares beforehand when using motorbike taxis.

Street Food: Vietnamese cuisine is famous worldwide. Try the local street food but ensure it's from clean and reputable vendors to avoid foodborne illnesses.

Language: English is not widely spoken outside major tourist areas. Learning a few basic Vietnamese phrases can be helpful and appreciated by locals.

Respect for Culture: Vietnam has a rich cultural heritage. Respect cultural sites, dress modestly when visiting temples, and ask for permission before taking photos of people.

Bargaining: Bargaining is common in markets and with street vendors. Start with a low offer and be prepared to negotiate to reach a fair price.

Safety: Vietnam is relatively safe for travellers, but be cautious of petty theft, scams, and traffic when crossing roads. Keep your belongings secure and be aware of your surroundings.

Internet Access: Purchase a local SIM card or portable Wi-Fi device for internet access during your stay. This can be especially useful for navigating and staying connected.

Explore Beyond Tourist Spots: While places like Hanoi, Ho Chi Minh City, and Ha Long Bay are popular, consider exploring off-the-beaten-path destinations for a more authentic experience.

Environmental Awareness: Be mindful of the environment. Avoid single-use plastics, support eco-friendly initiatives, and leave natural areas as you find them.

Travel Insurance: Consider purchasing travel insurance that covers medical emergencies, trip cancellations, and lost/stolen belongings for added peace of mind.

Guideline on how to plan an alternate tour of Vietnam in 8 days

One can plan an alternative tour plan opposite to my one. Planning a tour of Vietnam in 8 days requires careful consideration to make the most of your time and experience the country's diverse offerings. Here's a guideline to help you plan your trip effectively:

Day 1 and Day 2: Hanoi

- Day 1: Arrive in Hanoi, Vietnam's capital city. Spend the day exploring the Old Quarter, Hoan Kiem Lake, and Ngoc Son Temple.
- Day 2: Visit historical sites like the Ho Chi Minh Mausoleum, Ho Chi Minh Museum, One Pillar Pagoda, and the Temple of Literature. Experience the local culture through a traditional water puppet show in the evening.

Day 3 and Day 4: Ha Long Bay

- Day 3: Travel to Ha Long Bay (about 3-4 hours from Hanoi). Take a cruise on the bay, explore limestone caves, kayak, and enjoy seafood onboard.
- Day 4: Continue exploring Ha Long Bay with activities like swimming, visiting floating villages, and admiring the stunning landscapes.

Day 5 and Day 6: Hoi An

- Day 5: Fly from Hanoi to Da Nang and transfer to Hoi An (around 30 minutes by car). Explore Hoi An Ancient Town, known for its well-preserved architecture, lantern-lit streets, and vibrant markets.
- Day 6: Take a cycling tour to nearby villages, visit the My Son Sanctuary (a UNESCO World Heritage site), and enjoy Hoi An's renowned cuisine.

Day 7 and Day 8: Ho Chi Minh City (Saigon)

- Day 7: Fly from Da Nang to Ho Chi Minh City (about 1.5 hours). Visit iconic landmarks such as the Reunification Palace, War Remnants Museum, Notre Dame Cathedral, and Ben Thanh Market.
- Day 8: Explore the Cu Chi Tunnels, a network of underground tunnels used during the Vietnam War. Optionally, take a Mekong Delta day trip to experience rural life and floating markets.

Additional Tips:

- **Transfer:** Book flights and transfers in advance for smoother travel.
- **Accommodation:** Choose centrally located hotels or homestays for convenience.
- **Activities:** Prioritize must-see attractions but

leave room for spontaneous exploration.

- **Food:** Sample local dishes at recommended eateries and try street food.
- **Budget:** Plan your expenses including meals, activities, and souvenirs.
- **Weather:** Check seasonal weather patterns and pack accordingly.
- **Travel Insurance:** Purchase travel insurance for peace of mind during your trip

- Adjust the itinerary based on your interests and travel pace. Vietnam offers a rich tapestry of culture, history, and natural beauty, ensuring a memorable journey!

About the Author

Spondon Ganguli

An author of several engaging books, including 'Forgotten Love Unforgotten Love,' 'Let Me Hold Your Hand,' 'Do Not Leave Me,' 'Whispers of Realms,' and 'Nightmare's Embrace,' Spondon Ganguli's creative journey extends beyond the written word, with a dynamic website, offering insight into his multifaceted talents as an educator and artist. Discover more about Spondon Ganguli's captivating world at *https://spondonganguli.com/*

www.ingramcontent.com/pod-product-compliance
Lightning Source LLC
LaVergne TN
LVHW041533070526
838199LV00046B/1646